STATS TO BLOW YOUR MIND

JUNIOR EDITION

STATS TO BLOW YOUR MIND, JUNIOR EDITION

This book may be ordered by mail from the publisher. Please include $5.99 for postage and handling. Please support your local bookseller first!

Books published by Cider Mill Press Book Publishers are available at special discounts for bulk purchases in the United States by corporations, institutions, and other organizations. For more information, please contact the publisher.

Applesauce Press is an imprint of
Cider Mill Press Book Publishers
"Where good books are ready for press"
PO Box 454
12 Spring Street
Kennebunkport, Maine 04046
Visit us online!
cidermillpress.com

Printed in China

Typography: Dazzle Unicase, Halcom, Marvin

1 2 3 4 5 6 7 8 9 0
First Edition

STATS TO BLOW YOUR MIND

JUNIOR EDITION

75 KID-FRIENDLY FACTS YOU WON'T BELIEVE ARE REAL

BY TIM RAYBORN

ILLUSTRATIONS BY REBECCA PRY

APPLESAUCE PRESS

KENNEBUNKPORT, MAINE

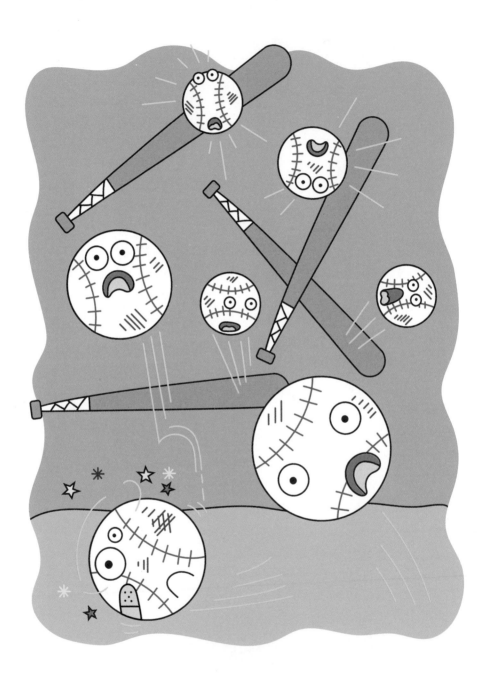

CONTENTS

INTRODUCTION

WHAT ARE STATISTICS?

Yes, they're numbers and, yes, that means math, but statistics can actually be really fun! Using statistics, researchers collect information about people, places, things, or pretty much anything, and look at what it might mean. They might want to learn how many people in Los Angeles eat chocolate ice cream every year, or how many people attended baseball games in June of the year 2019.

Knowing this kind of information can be very helpful to businesses, social studies, scientists, and other groups. An ice cream company might be able to see how much chocolate ice cream it sells in June 2019, and see if it's more or less than in 2018, or 2020, for example, and learn what it needs to do better to sell more. Major League Baseball can learn a lot about how popular their games are by seeing who is actually showing up at stadiums for them, and if they need to advertise better, lower ticket prices, or do any other things to get more fans to come to games.

So, a lot of statistical information is pretty regular stuff, even a little bit boring. It finds out things like, "23% of people bought new underwear last month." But there are also people and places that study weird and unusual statistics, the kind that can blow your mind. And that's what's in this little book. In each of these short chapters, you'll read about a whole lot of unusual numbers and discover just what a weird and wild world (and universe) we live in! You'll learn about how many Earths could fit inside of our sun, how much the most valuable Pokémon card is, how long you'll probably sleep over your whole life, and just how many teeth a snail has (yes, they have teeth!). Plus a whole lot more!

So pick a subject you're interested in, and dive in. You'll learn some surprising and fun new stuff that you can amaze your friends with and maybe stump your teachers. Statistics are actually really cool when they look at weird things like what's in this book, and you'll be amazed at what you'll discover in the following pages!

GAMES AND SPORTS

IN 1962, BASKETBALL STAR WILT CHAMBERLAIN SCORED 100 POINTS IN A SINGLE NBA GAME.

Wilt Chamberlain was one of the greatest basketball players of all time, and on March 2, 1962, he really got a chance to prove it! His team, the Philadelphia Warriors, was playing the New York Knicks. Wilt had an incredible game, scoring his last points with only 1 minute left! He broke the old record, which was also his, of 78 points. The Warriors went on to win the game 169-147, which is an amazingly high score for both teams!

THE TYPICAL BASEBALL LASTS FOR ABOUT 5 TO 7 PITCHES BEFORE IT NEEDS TO BE EXCHANGED FOR A NEW ONE.

In the major leagues, baseballs have a very short life. The general rule is that when they are hit by a bat, or hit the ground, they need to be replaced. Let's face it, baseballs take a beating, and teams only want fresh ones at all times. So on average, it take 5 to 7 pitches or less for a baseball to be "worn out" and ready to replace. Don't worry, all these old baseballs are used in batting practice or even sent to minor league teams, so it's not like they get wasted.

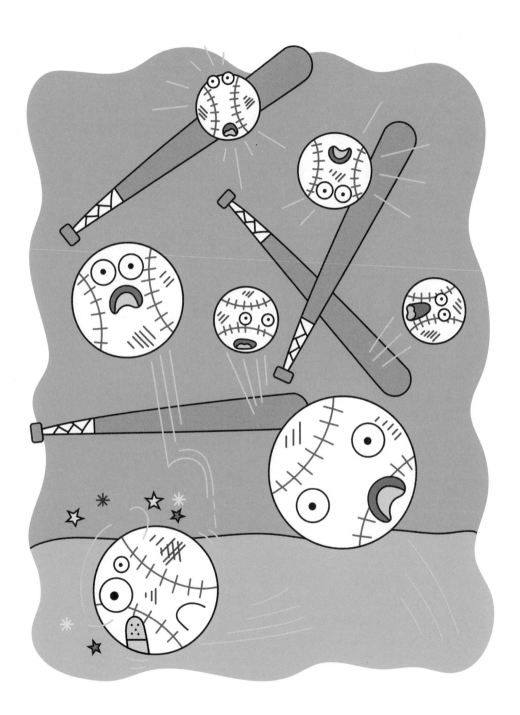

THE CHILDREN'S BOARD GAME CANDY LAND STILL SELLS OVER 1 MILLION COPIES A YEAR.

Candy Land is a fun game that most of us have played at time or other. Kids love it, and even adults think it's fun! You might be surprised to learn that it is one of the best-selling board games ever. It first appeared way back in 1949 and was a big hit almost right away. And it still is. Candy Land still sells an amazing 1 million copies around the world every year!

1 million copies sold A YEAR!

6 OF THE MOST COMMON LEGO BRICKS (WITH 8 STUDS) CAN BE COMBINED IN NEARLY 1 BILLION WAYS—915,103,765 WAYS, IN FACT!

Legos are awesome because you can put them together in so many ways. *So many ways.* A mathematician named Søren Eilers decided to try to figure out just how many ways the 6 basic bricks could fit together, so he wrote a computer program to figure it out. It took the computer a week to do it. It came up with an amazingly huge number: 915,103,765. And if you add more bricks, that number just gets bigger and bigger, and takes a computer even longer.

THE ORIGINAL RUBIK'S CUBE HAS 43 QUINTILLION POSSIBLE CONFIGURATIONS.

Rubik's Cube has been an amazing and super-hard puzzle ever since it was invented back in the 1970s. Millions of people have spent countless hours trying to get the cube's colors back into place, once they're mixed up. And there's a reason that it's so hard. It's been calculated that the original cube has over 43 quintillion possible combinations, or to be exact, 43,252,003,274,489,856,000! With a number like that, it's amazing that anyone ever solves it at all!

EACH SINGLE BASEBALL GAME HAS 12,386,344 POSSIBLE PLAYS.

Baseball games last a few hours and go on for at least 9 innings (unless it's a tie). That's kind of a normal length for a typical big league sports match (baseball, football, etc.), but because of all the ways the game can be played, all the possible hits, outs, runs, home runs, and everything else, when a baseball game starts, there are well over 12 million possible plays that can happen. But they can't happen all in a single game, of course!

THE ACTUAL AMOUNT OF ACTION/PLAYING TIME IN THE AVERAGE BASEBALL GAME IS BETWEEN ABOUT 14 AND 18 MINUTES, EVEN IF THE GAME LASTS ABOUT 3 HOURS.

It seems like there's a lot of standing around in baseball games, with batters waiting for pitches, pitchers trying to freak out batters, managers coming out to the pitcher's mound to talk with pitchers, and whole teams standing by, hoping for some action. And if you think this, you're right. The *Wall Street Journal* newspaper studied a lot of baseball games a few years ago and figured out that there are only about 18 minutes of action per game. Other studies have said it's even less. It's a sport where most players just stand around, but people still love watching it.

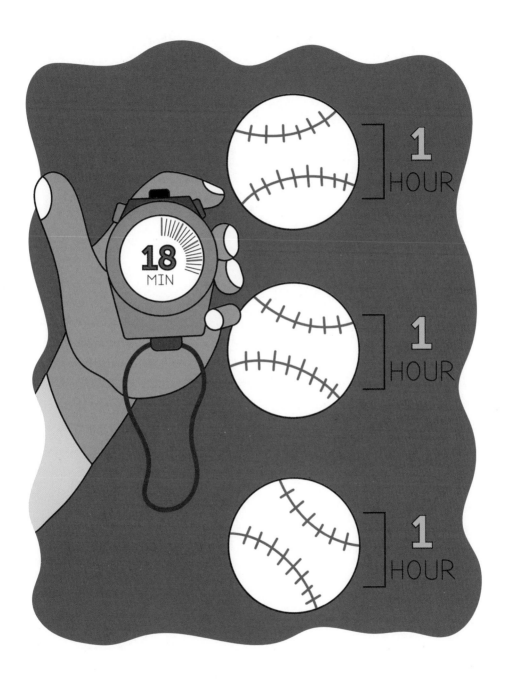

3 OLYMPIC GAMES HAVE BEEN HELD IN COUNTRIES THAT NO LONGER EXIST.

The Olympics (both winter and summer) are a big deal for each host country. These games happen every 4 years, bringing together the best athletes from around the world, and they've been doing it since the games were revived back in 1896. But of all the countries around the world that have hosted the games, 3 no longer exist: the Soviet Union (summer games in 1980), West Germany (summer games in 1972), and Yugoslavia (winter games in 1984). These countries were all affected by the changes to the world map in the late 1980s, when the Soviet Union fell apart, and none of them exist as those nations now.

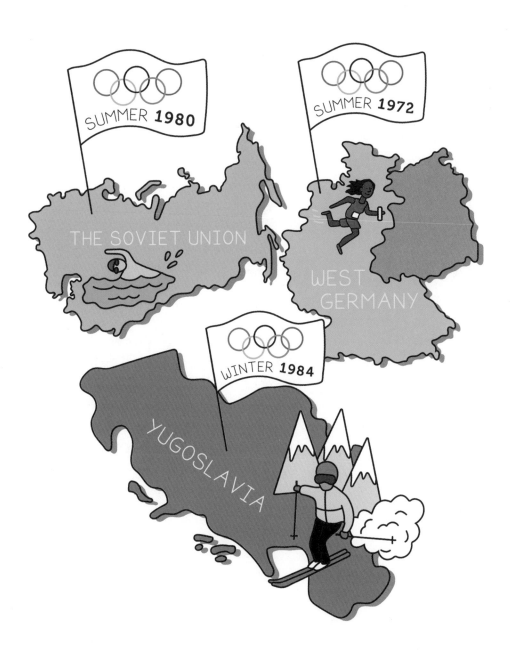

THE AVERAGE BASKETBALL PLAYER RUNS 2-3 MILES PER GAME.

Unlike baseball and even NFL football, where the players seem to spend a lot of time standing around waiting for something to happen, basketball is a very action-oriented game. Players are running almost constantly once the clock starts. Various studies have tried to figure out how far a typical basketball player runs in a game, and it usually comes out to about 2 and a half miles, sometimes a bit more, sometimes a bit less, but it's a lot of running.

THE AVERAGE SOCCER PLAYER RUNS 7-9 MILES PER GAME.

Forget basketball, soccer (known as "football" everywhere but the United States) has much larger numbers when it comes to miles run by players. The playing field is huge, after all! Plus, the players are running almost constantly up and down the field, and in most cases, they aren't substituted out for others, so any given player can be in for the while 90-minute match. All of this means that soccer/football players run more than players of almost any other competitive team sport, between 7 and 9 miles per game.

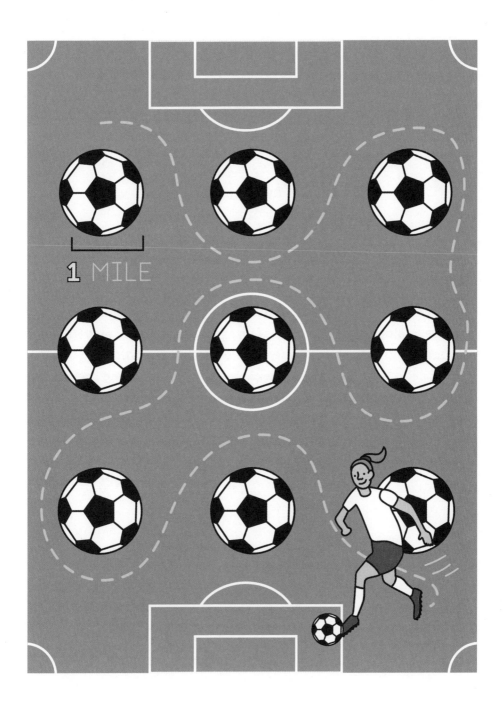

1 MILE

GOLF BALLS CAN REACH A SPEED OF UP TO 170 MILES PER HOUR.

While golf is another game with a lot of standing around and slow walking from place to place, those golf balls can really soar! Master players want to get a good swing in to start off, because obviously, they're trying to get the ball as close to the hole as possible. Some golfers can swing their clubs at up to 115 miles per hour, which means that after it's been hit, that tiny golf ball can soar through the air at over 170 miles per hour. Some golfers have clocked speeds of up to 190 miles per hour! They need those kinds of speeds if they're hoping to make a hole in one.

IN A PITCH, THE AVERAGE MAJOR LEAGUE BASEBALL ROTATES 15 TIMES BEFORE BEING HIT.

MLB pitchers pitch their baseballs fast and hard. Those balls can easily travel at over 90 miles per hour, right toward the batter. You'd better be kind of brave and very good at batting if you want to have a chance of hitting that ball! But pitchers also put spin on the balls when they release them (they need to do that for a curve ball, for example). It's estimated that in the very short time between a baseball leaving a pitcher's hand and it being hit by the batter or caught by the catcher, it will spin at least 15 times. Next time you watch a baseball pitch, try to imagine that!

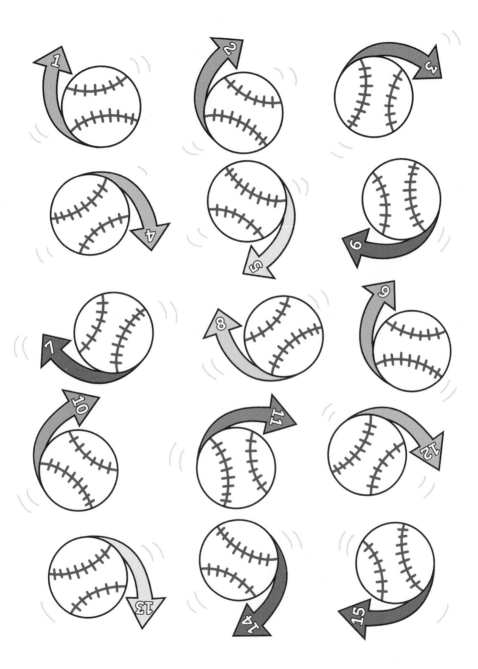

PING-PONG (TABLE TENNIS) BALLS CAN GO AS FAST AS 70 MILES PER HOUR WHEN HIT.

Ping-Pong is a fun indoor game, a mini version of tennis where players hit a very light and small ball over the table at each other. But for professional, competitive players, Ping-Pong is anything but fun and easy. Those people can offer up some nasty serves that are meant to try to make the other player miss as badly as possible. The tiny Ping-Pong ball can reach up to 70 miles per hour in a professional serve, which is amazingly fast for something barely weighs anything!

BEFORE 1900, BOXING MATCHES COULD LAST UP TO 100 ROUNDS.

Boxing is still a popular sport, but it makes a lot of people worry about the safety of the boxers. And that's just these days, when matches only go 12 rounds. In the nineteenth century, boxing matches could be absolutely brutal. They could go on literally for hours. In 1893, a match in New Orleans started at 9:00 p.m. and was still going on over 7 hours later! It went for 110 rounds before the referee decided to call the match and told the boxers to split the prize money. One of them had broken both of his hands. There are stories of other matches going 75 rounds or more. So, only having 12 now seems like a very good idea!

IN A HORSE RACE, THE HORSE FAVORED TO WIN ONLY WINS ABOUT 35% OF THE TIME, OR EVEN LESS.

Horse racing is a very popular sport for people to watch, and they often like to bet on which horse will win. In any race, there will be horses that are more likely to win than others. These are called the favorites. And of these, there is probably one horse who people think has the best chance of winning. So people like to bet that these horses will win. But surprisingly, these favorite horses usually only win about one-third of the time, or less. And that's why it's called gambling; you never know what will happen!

THE MAJOR LEAGUE BASEBALL TEAMS USE ABOUT 900,000 BASEBALLS EACH SEASON.

We've already seen how a baseball doesn't stay around in play very long. As soon as it's hit or gets scuffed on the ground, it's replaced with a new ball, and the old ones are used for practice or sent to the minor leagues. What that means is that the MLB teams go through a whole lot of new baseballs in a single season. It's thought to be about 900,000 balls, used by all of the teams together. That's a huge number of baseballs, and it keeps baseball makers very busy!

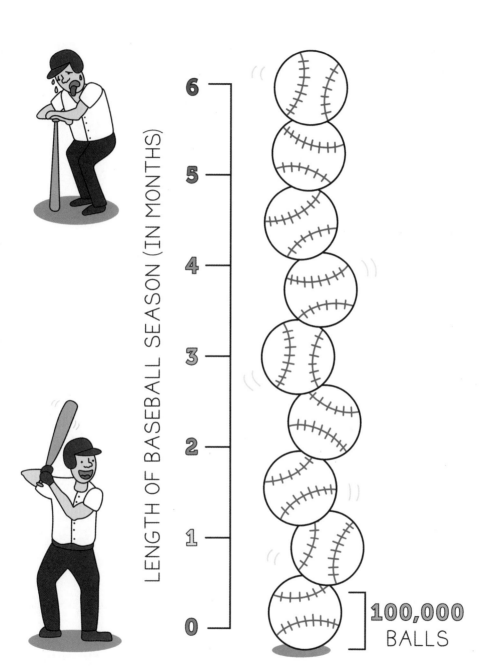

LENGTH OF BASEBALL SEASON (IN MONTHS)

6
5
4
3
2
1
0

100,000
BALLS

SURGEONS WHO PLAY VIDEO GAMES FOR AT LEAST 3 HOURS A WEEK WORK 27% FASTER AND MAKE 37% FEWER MISTAKES.

You probably know that video games can make you faster and more alert, since you have to keep an eye out for all kinds of challenges, no matter what game you're playing. An interesting study found that surgeons who play games for a few hours a week do a lot better when it's time for them to perform their surgeries. They make fewer mistakes and get the job done faster, because they've been training their hands and eyes with video games. So, just remember that when you're gaming, you could actually be training to be a surgeon!

TOYS

THE WORLD'S MOST EXPENSIVE TOY IS THE ASTOLAT DOLLHOUSE CASTLE, WHICH IS WORTH ABOUT $8.5 MILLION.

This amazing dollhouse is like no other one in the world. It has 7 floors and 29 separate rooms, is 9 feet tall, and weighs about 800 pounds. There is a ballroom, a kitchen (with tiny doll foods!), a basement, a library (with tiny doll books), hallways, and much more. Of course, this incredible house was not created to play with; it was made by an artist named Elaine Diehl, who started building it in 1974. It took her 13 years to finish it, and it has over 10,000 parts inside, some of which are made of silver and gold!

FOR SALE

7 FLOORS

29 ROOMS

$$ MORE THAN YOUR ALLOWANCE

McDONALD'S IS THE WORLD'S BIGGEST TOY DISTRIBUTOR, AT 1.5 BILLION TOYS A YEAR.

When you think of toy companies, you might think of businesses like Hasbro and Mattel. And it's true, those companies are huge and sell hundreds of millions of toys every year. But if you want to know the biggest toy seller in the world is, it's actually McDonalds. The McDonalds Happy Meal always includes a small toy with each meal. And all those toys add up to an absolutely huge number, 1.5 billion! That's how many Happy Meals are sold every year, so that's how many toys are sold with them. It's amazing to think that a fast-food restaurant outsells the big toy companies, but it's true!

BY 2020, TOYS AND GAMES SOLD ABOUT $275 BILLION AROUND THE WORLD.

Let's face it, toys and games are really popular, and for the companies that make them, they make an amazing amount of money. If you add up all the money made in 2020 by every toy and game company in the world, it comes out to an incredible $275 billion! People sure love their games and toys, and the companies that make them love those people. The thing is, this number is only going to get bigger over the next few years. It's a great time to be a toy company!

THE 1999 FIRST EDITION SHADOWLESS HOLOGRAPHIC CHARIZARD #4, A RARE POKÉMON CARD, SOLD FOR $369,000 IN DECEMBER, 2020.

Pokémon cards are colorful, cool, and it turns out, they can be really valuable. What makes something worth more is how hard it is to find (that's true of cards, comics, and other collectibles). The 1999 First Edition Shadowless Holographic Charizard is a very rare card, so if you have one in great condition, you're really lucky. In late 2020, this single card sold to a collector for an incredible $369,000! It's said to be one of the cards fans want most, so it's very hard to get. Good luck finding one!

$9,000
+
$10,000
+
$50,000
+
$100,000
+
$100,000
+
$100,000

= $369,000

MOST OF THE WORLD'S TOYS (ABOUT 80%) ARE MADE IN CHINA.

China is a very big and very busy country, with a lot of people and a lot of factories that employ them. China makes a huge amount of things for the world, and one of those things is toys. This includes everything from electronic toys to dolls, games, plastic, and old-fashioned wooden toys. Some people even call China the "new North Pole" because so many toys are made there! People who have studied this think China will only make more in the future. And with all the kids in the world, Santa needs all the help he can get!

IT'S THOUGHT THAT AROUND THE WORLD, MORE THAN 12 BILLION TOYS ARE SOLD EVERY YEAR.

In the United States alone, over 3 billion toys are sold every year. The worldwide number of 12 million is a little harder to figure out, but this seems like a good guess (people that do math like to figure out these things). That's an incredible number of toys! And it looks like the number is only going to grow over the next 10 years, since the demand for toys shows no sign of slowing down.

THE UNITED STATES HAS A LITTLE OVER 4% OF THE WORLD'S POPULATION, BUT BUYS OVER 40% OF THE WORLD'S TOYS.

The U.S. has a lot of people, but compared to the number of people in the rest of the world, its population is pretty tiny. Only about 4.25% of all the people in the world live in the U.S. But that doesn't mean that we don't have a big impact on the toy world! In fact, it seems that about 40% of all the toys made in the world are bought and played with by American kids. That's an amazingly large number! Kids in other parts of the world just don't have as many toys.

BARBIE DOLLS SELL IN HUGE NUMBERS EVERY YEAR, OVER 100 EVERY MINUTE.

Mattel is one of the biggest toy companies in the world, and Barbie dolls are almost always its biggest sellers. The dolls and accessories have been super popular ever since they first appeared back in 1959. These days, Mattel is selling 58 million dolls around the world each year. That's more than 100 dolls every minute! Barbies are sold in at least 150 countries around the world, and the Barbie YouTube channel has over 5 million subscribers. Barbie is a force to be reckoned with and isn't going away anytime soon!

60
SECONDS

10 DOLLS

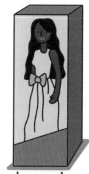

10 DOLLS

10 DOLLS

10 DOLLS

10 DOLLS

10 DOLLS

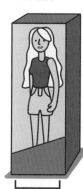

10 DOLLS

10 DOLLS

10 DOLLS

10 DOLLS

LEGO IS ACTUALLY THE WORLD'S BIGGEST TIRE MANUFACTURER.

When you think of tires, you think of the ones that go on cars. They're made by companies like Goodyear and Michelin. So you'd probably guess that when you're thinking about who makes them most tires in years, it's going to be one of those businesses, right? Nope. The biggest tire maker in the world is Lego, which in 2010, made about 381 *million* tires for its toys! That number has only gotten much bigger over the last 10 years, with some reports putting it as high as 700 million. Okay, these are not exactly the same as tires made for full-sized cars and trucks, but it's still an amazing number when you think about it.

THE AVERAGE CHILD GOES THROUGH 730 CRAYONS BY THE AGE OF 10.

Let's face it, we all love coloring! Adults still do it a lot, too! There is something so nice about opening a box of new crayons and getting to work on your latest art project. There's no doubt about it, crayons are popular, especially with kids. Just how popular? Well, people who have studied that question have figured out that the average kid will use up about 730 crayons by the time they are 10 years old, in all different colors and box sizes. That's amazing! Have *you* used that many so far? Try keeping count!

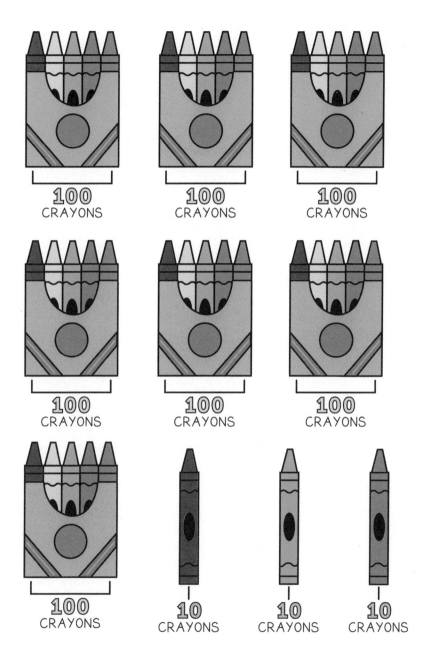

100
CRAYONS

100
CRAYONS

100
CRAYONS

100
CRAYONS

100
CRAYONS

100
CRAYONS

100
CRAYONS

10
CRAYONS

10
CRAYONS

10
CRAYONS

THE LEGO COMPANY HAS MADE OVER 400 BILLION BRICKS SINCE 1958.

Lego pretty much rules the world, and with a number like this, you can see why! People just can't get enough of their Legos, and they buy billions of them every year all around the world. With more than 400 billion bricks made in the last 60 years, that's enough that each person on Earth could have 62 bricks. Of course, if everyone only had 62 bricks, they wouldn't be able to build many cool things, but it still gives you an idea of just how many bricks there are in the world!

HISTORY

HISTORIANS THINK THAT ABOUT 97% OF HISTORY HAS BEEN LOST TO US.

What that means is that for most of our history as human beings, we had no ways of writing things down. Writing was probably invented in the Middle East over 5,000 years ago, and then again in China and in Central America. This meant that people could finally write down stories, history, and anything else they wanted to, and preserve it for the future. But 5,000 years ago is a very short time, considering that modern humans have been around for about 200,000 years. There are some really amazing cave paintings and rock carvings that are much older than writing (40,000 to 50,000 years), but they show us pictures, not words. So most of what happened to humans before writing began has to be figured out by archaeologists and scientists. And sadly, most of it we will never know.

ALEXANDER THE GREAT NAMED AT LEAST 70 CITIES FOR HIMSELF.

Alexander the Great (356-323 BCE) was one of the world's great military leaders. His armies marched across the Middle East and even into India, and he conquered huge amounts of territory. One of the things he liked to do was order the building of new cities (which often started as military forts), and he named more than 70 of them after himself! Alexandria in modern Egypt, is probably the most famous of these. He even named a city in what is now Pakistan after his favorite horse! Yes, he was pretty conceited, but considering how much land he took over before he died at the young age of 32, he was pretty impressive.

THE CIRCUS MAXIMUS IN ANCIENT ROME COULD HOLD BETWEEN 150,000 AND 250,000 PEOPLE AT ANY ONE TIME.

The Circus Maximus had nothing to do with clowns or show animals (though animals were featured sometimes). It was a giant sports stadium in the city of Rome, built about 2,500 years ago. The big event at the Circus Maximus was chariot racing, which was kind of like modern car racing, except it was done with small chariots pulled by horses. The crowds loved it! There were also gladiator fights and other sports matches. The most amazing thing was how many people the stadium could hold, up to 250,000. That's a quarter of a million people in one place!

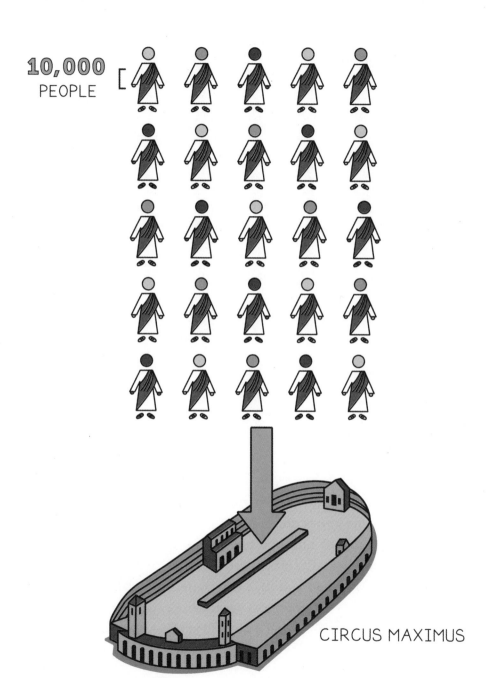

10,000
PEOPLE

CIRCUS MAXIMUS

CLEOPATRA LIVED CLOSER TO OUR TIME (ABOUT 2,000 YEARS AFTER HER) THAN TO THE BUILDING OF THE PYRAMIDS (ABOUT 2,500 YEARS BEFORE HER).

Cleopatra was a famous queen in Egypt, who lived when the Romans were really starting to gain power and transform themselves into an empire. We think of her as living a long time ago, and she did, but actually she is closer in time to us than she was to the great pyramids at Giza (the ones just outside of modern Cairo). They had already been there for 2,500 years when she became queen. It will be another 500 years before we're as far away in time from her as they were. It gives you a good idea of just how old Egypt and it civilization are!

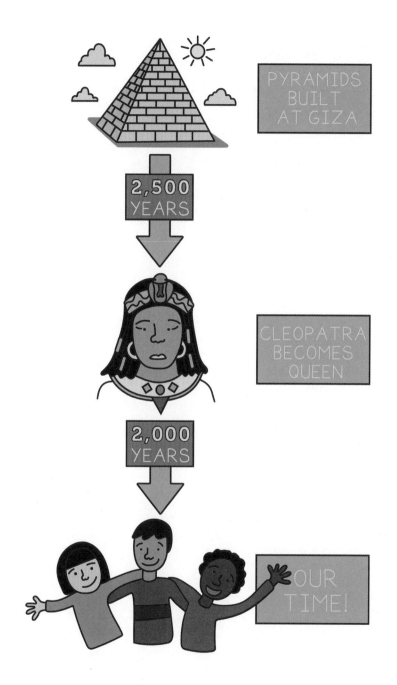

PYRAMIDS BUILT AT GIZA

2,500 YEARS

CLEOPATRA BECOMES QUEEN

2,000 YEARS

OUR TIME!

THE GREAT PYRAMID HAS OVER 2.3 MILLION STONE BLOCKS.

The Great Pyramid is huge! Like, really big. It's about **481 feet (147 meters)** tall at the top, and it was built with something like 2.3 million blocks of stone in various sizes, which can weigh up to 15 tons. It was built by the pharaoh Khufu, beginning in about 2550 BCE, and took about 20 years to complete. It wasn't built by slaves, though. The laborers who worked on the pyramid were often seasonal (meaning they had other jobs at different times of the year), lived in housing nearby that was built for them, and were paid for their work.

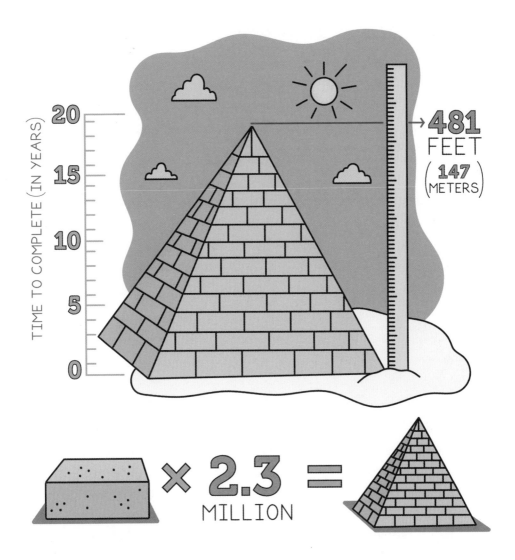

TIME TO COMPLETE (IN YEARS)

20
15
10
5
0

481 FEET
(147 METERS)

× 2.3 MILLION =

PRESIDENTS JOHN ADAMS AND THOMAS JEFFERSON BOTH DIED ON THE SAME DAY–JULY 4– 50 YEARS AFTER THE FIRST INDEPENDENCE DAY IN 1776.

Adams and Jefferson were the second and third presidents of the United States. They were friends but also rivals who often disagreed strongly with each other. Jefferson died first, on July 4, 1826, just before 1:00 p.m. at his home in Virginia. The same day, Adams was also dying at his home in Massachusetts. It's said that his last words were "Thomas Jefferson still survives," not knowing that Jefferson had passed away only a few hours earlier. Interestingly, another president, James Monroe, also died on July 4, exactly 5 years after Jefferson and Adams!

THE KRAKATOA VOLCANIC ERUPTION IN 1883 WAS HEARD THOUSANDS OF MILES AWAY.

Krakatoa was a volcano on an island in Indonesia. On August 27, 1883, it violently erupted, making the loudest known noise in modern history. It was heard in Perth, Australia, about 2,800 miles away, and damaged the eardrums of sailors who were in boats more than 40 miles away from the eruption. The sound waves from the eruption traveled around the Earth 4 times. The force of the eruption caused waves that were felt as far away as South Africa, and even mini waves in the English Channel. It spewed ash 50 miles up into the air that filtered the sunlight so much that people in New York thought fires had started when they saw the sunsets. It was a terrifying reminder of the power of nature.

ASH SPEWED
50
MILES INTO
THE AIR

IT DAMAGED THE
EARS OF SAILORS
40 MILES AWAY

IT WAS HEARD
IN AUSTRAILIA
2,800
MILES AWAY

SOUND WAVES TRAVELED
AROUND THE WORLD
4 TIMES

WAVES REACHED
SOUTH AFRICA
AND EVEN
THE ENGLISH CHANNEL

IN ITALY IN 1861, ONLY ABOUT 2.5% OF ITALIANS ACTUALLY SPOKE ITALIAN.

This might seem like a truly weird statistic, but it's true. Italy was only united as a single country in 1861. Before that, it had been many smaller countries, and each of those had its own version of the Italian language. Some of these were very different from others. This was actually true in many other countries in Europe, such as Spain and France. People in different parts of the country spoke different dialects of the same language or completely different languages of their own and couldn't understand each other. So when Italy united as a country, only about 1 in 40 people spoke the language that we now call Italian. It took a long time for it to be spoken nationwide.

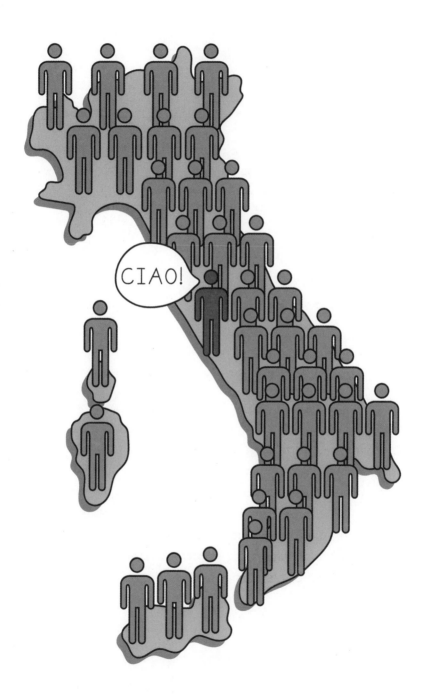

ABRAHAM LINCOLN WAS A WRESTLER WHO ONLY LOST 1 MATCH OUT OF 300.

Most people know that Abraham Lincoln was the U.S. president during the American Civil War, and that he was assassinated in 1865, just as the war was ending. You might know that he lived in a log cabin as a child and was sometimes called "Honest Abe." But most people don't know that he was a wrestler before becoming president, and a very good one! In 12 years of wrestling, he was said to have faced at least 300 opponents, and there is only one record of him losing; that's pretty amazing! Lincoln even used his wrestling past as part of his presidential campaign, to show that he could handle tough situations.

SCIENCE

YOU FART BETWEEN 14 AND 23 TIMES A DAY.

Yeah, okay, stop giggling. The fact is that farting is not only normal and necessary, but it's also a sign that your digestive system is in good health. When you eat food, your body breaks it down in your intestines, and when this happens, it naturally releases gasses. You also swallow a lot of air when eating (this can also come up with burps). So farting allows your body to release those gasses and it usually makes you feel better, because it relives the pressure. So don't worry if you fart many times throughout the day!

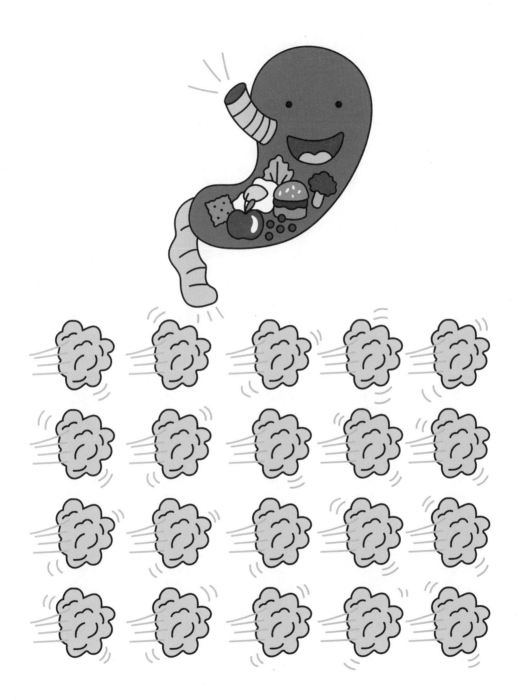

THERE ARE 31,536,000 SECONDS IN A SINGLE YEAR.

That's a lot of seconds! It's calculated by 60 seconds times 60 minutes, times 24 hours, times 365 days. Actually how many seconds there are in a year also depends on which calendar you use. Technically, 1 year is about 365.2425 days (which is why we have an extra day every 4 years in leap year). And if we go by that number, there are 31,556,952 seconds. Either way, it's a huge number of seconds, always ticking by...

20% OF ALL THE OXYGEN YOU BREATHE IN IS USED BY YOUR BRAIN.

Brains are amazing. They pretty much never turn off, even when we're asleep (which is why we dream, among other things). But because they're always running, they need a lot of energy to keep going. And that comes from oxygen, the oxygen that we breathe in. In fact, our brains are only about 2% of our whole body mass, but they need up to 20% of the oxygen we breathe in order to keep working. So, the air you breathe keeps you going in more ways than one!

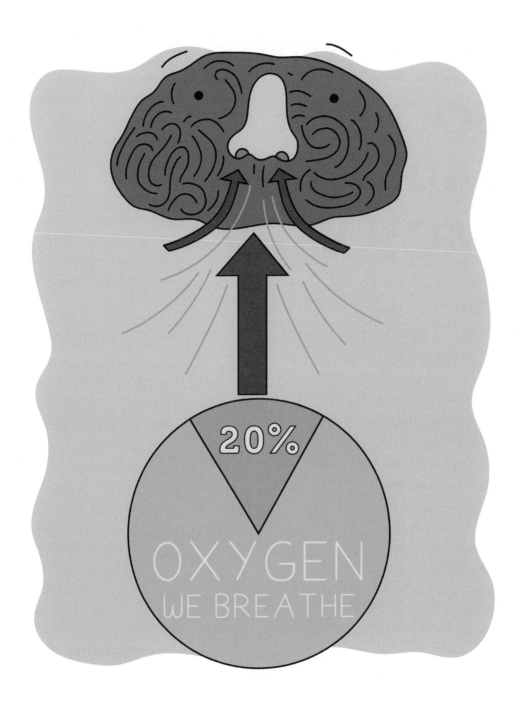

THE EARTH HAS 500,000 EARTHQUAKES EACH YEAR.

The Earth is a very active planet: earthquakes, shifting continents, tectonic plates, volcanos... things are always moving underground! Volcanic eruptions, the movement of the plates, and fault lines can all cause earthquakes, pretty much all the time. What that means is that there about a half million earthquakes all over the world every year! About one-fifth, or 100,000, of these are earthquakes which we can feel (the rest can only be picked up by sensitive equipment), and of those, only about 100 of these will actually cause some damage to buildings or the Earth's surface. It's good that so few cause destruction, but that's still a lot of earthquakes that can!

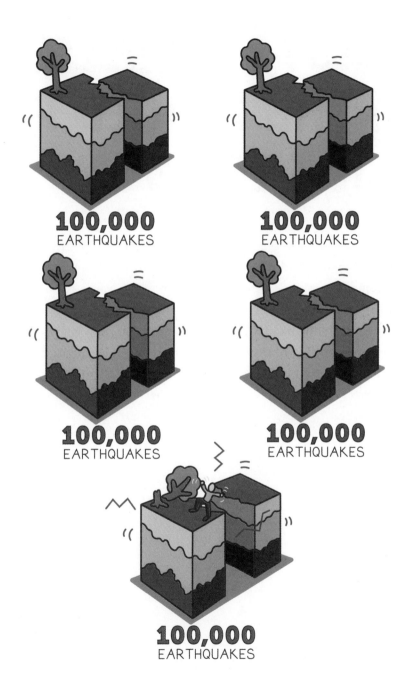

100,000
EARTHQUAKES

100,000
EARTHQUAKES

100,000
EARTHQUAKES

100,000
EARTHQUAKES

100,000
EARTHQUAKES

ABOUT 1.3 MILLION EARTHS COULD FIT INSIDE THE SUN.

Our sun is the big deal in our solar system. You could say it's the "star" of the show (bad joke!). And it's pretty big, compared to the Earth, that is. If we could make enough copies of the Earth in the same size, we would need 1.3 million of them, all grouped together to equal the size of our sun. It's hard to imagine something that big, but the thing is, our sun isn't even all that large, compared to a lot of other stars. A star called UY Scuti, a hypergiant near the middle of the Milky Way Galaxy, is so big that it is larger than the orbit of Jupiter around our own sun! It's almost impossible to even imagine something that big.

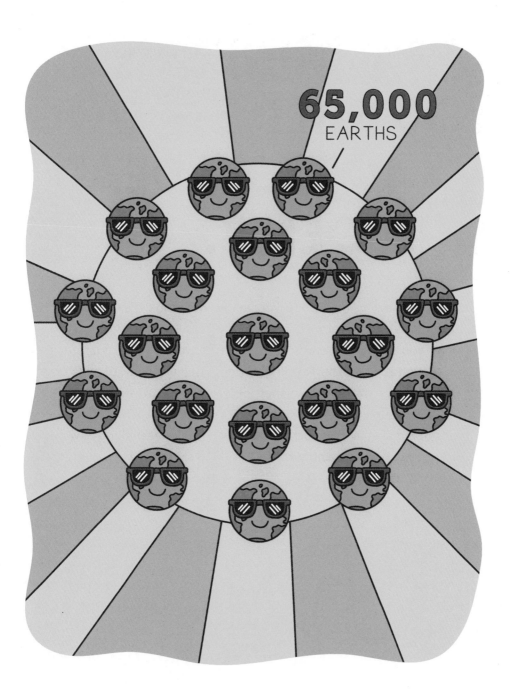

65,000
EARTHS

EACH MINUTE, YOU SHED 30,000 TO 40,000 DEAD SKIN CELLS.

Your skin is amazing, and while you might not think it's doing much, it's very important. It's the largest organ of the body, and it keeps out harmful infections and protects your insides from all sorts of intruders. It might look as though it's just there, doing nothing, being a wall. But it's actually very active. Every minute, your shed between 30,000 and 40,000 dead skin cells, as the skin regrows and repairs itself. That works out to about 9 pounds of old skin every year! But your skin is always making new cells, so don't worry, you won't disappear! All that dead skin tends to become dust in your house, by the way.

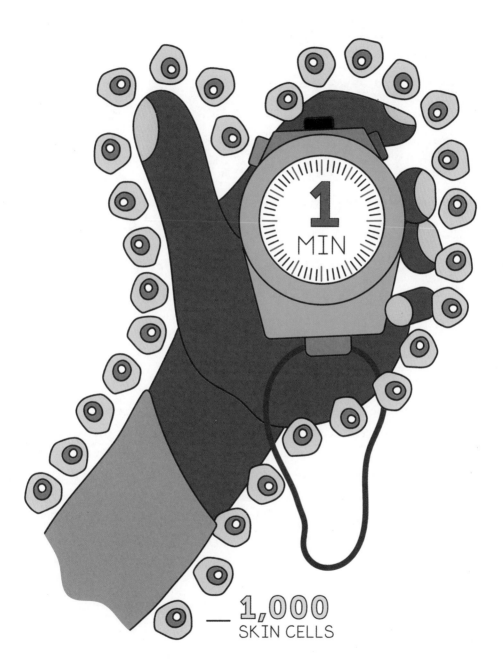

1 MIN

— 1,000 SKIN CELLS

THERE ARE BETWEEN 10 AND 30 MILLION DIFFERENT SPECIES OF INSECTS ON OUR PLANET.

You might like bugs; you might hate them. They can be really cool or kind of creepy. You'll probably see more of them in the summer than in in winter (except for ants!), and you probably know that they are all around us all the time. Scientists who study insects, known as entomologists, have discovered about 1 million different species of insects around the world. But most think that there are more, a *lot* more. If they are right, then there might be 10 to 30 *million* more species of insects in the world that we haven't found yet. Bugs truly rule the Earth!

BETWEEN 10 -AND- 30 MILLION

DIFFERENT SPECIES OF BUGS!

IF YOU COULD DRIVE A CAR STRAIGHT UP INTO THE AIR, IT WOULD ONLY TAKE ABOUT 1 HOUR TO DRIVE TO SPACE.

Let's say you have a magic car that can drive straight up into the sky, escaping Earth's gravity, and you can go at about 60 miles per hour. It would only take you a little under an hour to reach the edge of the Earth's atmosphere. The atmosphere has 4 layers: the troposphere, the stratosphere, the mesosphere, and the thermosphere at the outer part. The thermosphere begins about 56 miles up, and while it's part of Earth's atmosphere, it's so thin that it's basically a part of space. So, you'd only need to drive for 56 minutes to reach it. That's how thin our protective atmosphere is!

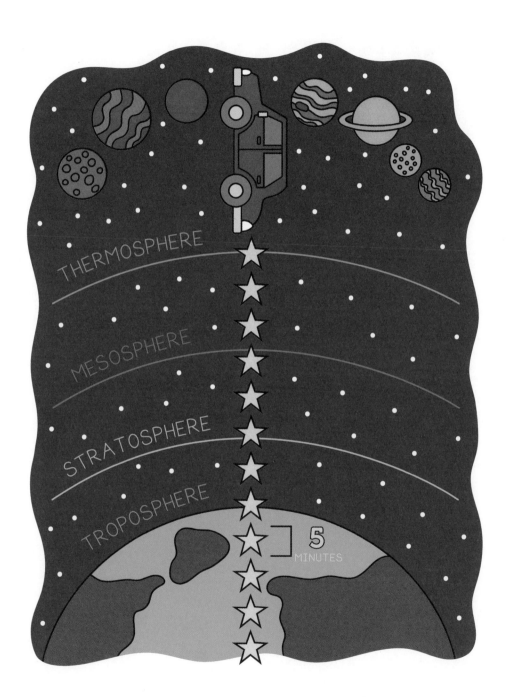

YOUR BRAIN IS MADE UP OF ABOUT 73% WATER.

You've already read that our brains need a huge amount of the oxygen that we breathe, but you might not know that our brains are also mostly water: 73%, or almost three-fourths of our brains are, in fact, good old water. If you don't drink enough water, you might find that your ability to concentrate and think gets worse. That's because your brain needs more water than it's getting and is struggling. So, keep your brain happy and drink plenty of water throughout the day!

73%—

THERE ARE ABOUT 2,000 THUNDERSTORMS ON PLANET EARTH EVERY MINUTE.

Thunderstorms can be amazing, loud, and scary. They can be really cool or even spooky on a rainy night. As you probably know, thunder is the sound that lightning makes, and often you will see the flash of lightning before you hear the thunder, because light travels much faster that sound. Earth is a very stormy place, and it's believed that there are about 2,000 thunderstorms going on somewhere in our atmosphere every *minute*. That's about 16 million thunderstorms every year!

THE UNITED STATES GETS OVER 1,200 TORNADOES EVERY YEAR.

The geographic shape of the United States means that it gets a large number of tornadoes every year, about 1,200! This is also because of the weather conditions in the center of the U.S., where tornadoes are most likely to happen (though they have been reported in all 50 states!). Certain times so year are more dangerous for tornadoes. Depending on the location, April to July are probably the worst months for tornadoes to happen. Not all of those 1,200 reach the ground, thankfully!

60
TORNADOES

A BOLT OF LIGHTNING IS UP TO 5 TIMES HOTTER THAN THE SURFACE OF THE SUN.

Actually, lightning itself doesn't have a temperature, but as it moves through the air, the air heats up to amazingly high temperatures. As lightning passes through air, it can heat it up to an incredible 50,000 degrees Fahrenheit, which is indeed 5 times hotter than the sun's surface (at about 10,000 degrees). Fortunately, this heat doesn't stay around long, but a bolt of lightning can still cause a lot of damage when it hits a house, a tree, or a person!

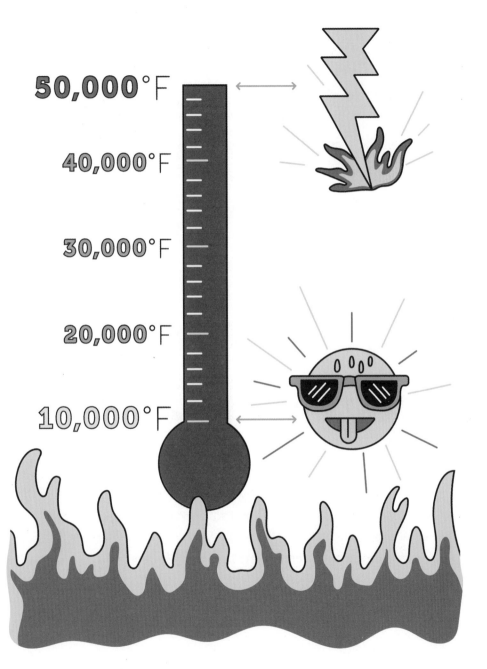

THE ASTRONAUTS' FOOTPRINTS ON THE MOON WILL STAY THERE FOR THE NEXT 100 MILLION YEARS, IF NOT LONGER.

The moon is amazing place that we first visited way back on July 20, 1969. But it's very different from Earth, with no atmosphere, no water, and no weather. What this means is that the footprints that the astronauts left on the moon will stay there for millions of years, unless a meteor or something slams into the moon and erases them. Some astronomers think that as long as that doesn't happen, these footprints will be there for as long as the moon exists!

100
MILLION
YEARS
LATER

TODAY

JULY 20,
1969

IF YOU COULD FLY IN AN AIRPLANE TO PLUTO, IT WOULD TAKE ABOUT 680 YEARS TO GET THERE.

If you've even been on an airplane flight, you know that they go pretty fast. A Boeing 777 can fly up to 590 miles an hour, but even so, a long trip, like Los Angeles to London, still takes almost 10 hours, and you can get really tired on the way. But what if you could get on a plane and fly to Pluto? Well, Pluto averages about 3.6 billion miles away from Earth (it can be much closer or much farther away, depending on its orbit), so if you could fly in the 777 at that speed, it would take you about 680 years to get there! Except, you never would get there, of course, because nobody lives that long. But it gives you a really good idea about just how huge our solar system is!

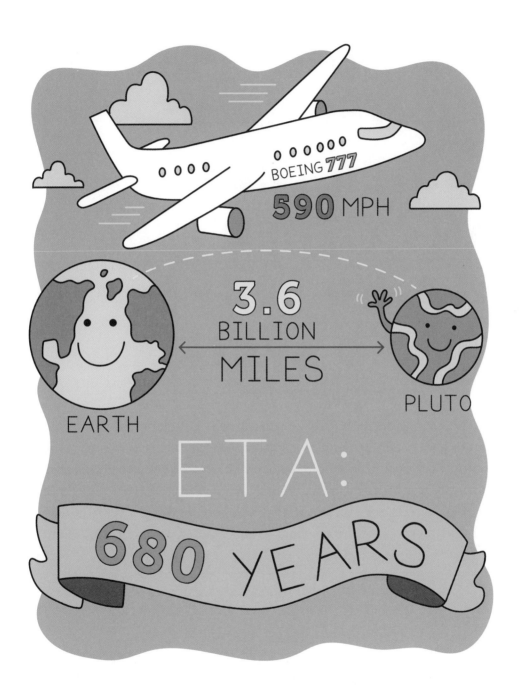

THE GIANT PLANET JUPITER SPINS FASTER THAN ANY OTHER PLANET IN THE SOLAR SYSTEM.

You might know that Jupiter is what's called a "gas giant." It's a huge planet (the largest in our system), made mostly of gasses, that has at least 79 moons, and even has rings. It also has the shortest days of any planet in the solar system. It takes the Earth around 24 hours to make 1 rotation (which is 1 day), but Jupiter makes its rotation in only about 9.5 hours. With its gigantic size, that means that it's spinning at its equator at about 28,000 miles per hour!

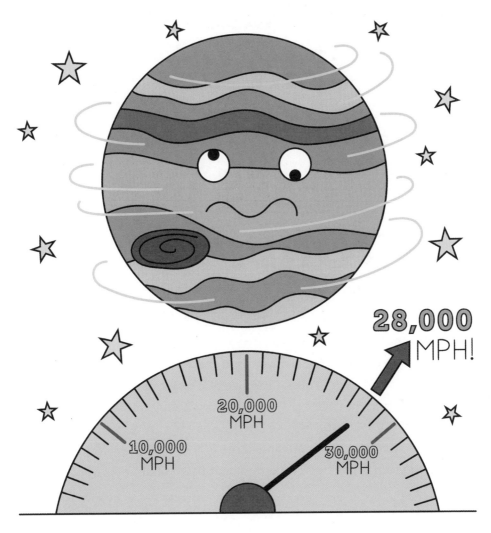

28,000 MPH!

10,000 MPH

20,000 MPH

30,000 MPH

SPIN-O-METER

A NEUTRON STAR CAN SPIN UP TO MORE THAN 700 TIMES IN 1 SECOND.

Neutron stars are strange things. They're not stars in the way we think of them, and definitely not like our sun. They are "born" when a larger star blows apart (in what's called a supernova), and the remaining part in the middle collapses on itself, down to about the size of a city, but heavier than our own sun. That core part of this star becomes very heavy and dense and begins spinning at a very fast rate. It's like Earth's spinning, only much, much faster. One neutron star, with the confusing name of PSR J1748-2446ad (good luck remembering that!), has been recorded as rotating 716 times per second!

700 SPINS PER SECOND

ANIMALS

A GARDEN SNAIL HAS 14,000 TEETH.

You've seen snails in gardens, in bushes, and all kinds of other places, especially after a good rain. They're slow, very slow, kind of cute, and they like to munch on plants. But how do they eat? Through little mouths of course. You just might not ever have noticed them before. Go look up a video online of a snail eating; it's pretty cool! But did you know that a typical snail has over 14,000 teeth? That's right! They're not like our teeth, but instead are tiny little spikes on its tongue (yes, snails have tongues, too!). These tiny teeth are what let them munch and chew up tasty plants, like those in your garden.

1,000
TEETH

WHALES SWALLOW ABOUT HALF A MILLION CALORIES IN EACH MOUTHFUL.

Whales of all kinds are huge, beautiful animals that swim gracefully through the ocean and delight whale watchers everywhere. As you can guess, animals this big need a *lot* of food. The majority of their food supply comes from a small sea creature called a krill. These shrimp-like animals swim in large groups, and a hungry whale comes by, opens its gigantic mouth and swallows huge number of them whole? How many? Well, larger whales, like the blue whale, can swallow up to 800 pounds (about 360 kg) of krill in one gulp! That's about half a million calories at a time!

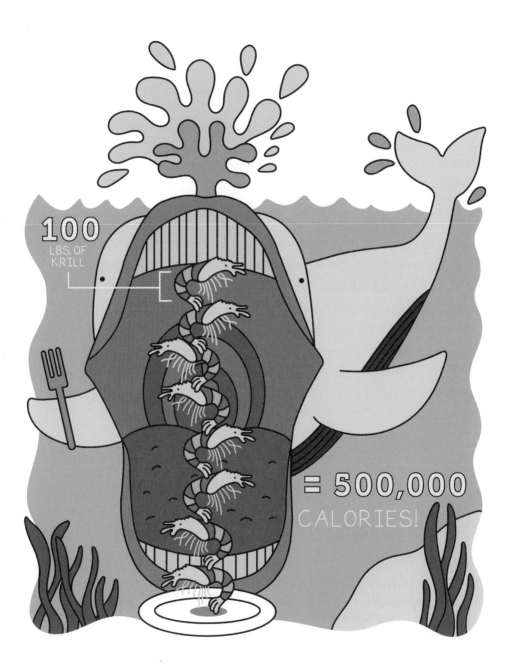

ELEPHANTS ARE PREGNANT FOR 22 MONTHS.

You probably know that a human baby takes 9 months to grow inside the mother. That's a long time, but some other animals have very different waits for their babies, all of them longer than humans: Camels are pregnant for between 13 and 15 months, rhinos carry theirs for 15 to 18 months, whales can be pregnant for between 17 and 19 months, and elephants can be pregnant for up to 22 months, almost 2 years! There are some animals that can go even longer. Some species of sharks give birth to live young, while others lay eggs. It's known that some shark species can be pregnant for three and a half years!

9 MONTHS

13-15 MONTHS

15-18 MONTHS

22 MONTHS

17-19 MONTHS

A SNAIL CAN SLEEP FOR UP TO 3 YEARS.

As you know, snails are slow. And not only that, they have a lot of teeth, as we've already seen. But did you know that a snail can take very long naps? Like, up to 3 years? It sounds incredible and hard to believe, but it's true. The thing is, they don't do this by choice. If a snail decides to hibernate for this long, it's usually because it is lacking enough moisture to move about and eat. This can happen in hot and dry weather, or even in cold and dry weather. It will find a safe place to sleep, excrete mucus to cover itself (gross!) and sleep until conditions are better. So if you see a snail that's not moving, don't assume that it's dead; it might just be having a very long slumber!

A DOG'S HEARING IS AT LEAST TWICE AS GOOD AS A HUMAN'S.

Our human ears are pretty good, but dogs are way better. You may have heard of the decibel system. That's a measure of how loud a sound it makes. Starting at 0 decibels, we can hear things that are very quiet up to things that are very loud, and things that are very deep tones, as well as very high-pitched tones. But a dog's hearing is much better than ours, up to twice as much better. Dogs can hear about twice as many sound frequencies as humans, and sounds that are 4 times as far away. That's why sometimes you'll notice your dog titling its head and listening. It's probably hearing something that you can't!

SOME REINDEER CAN WALK MORE THAN 3,000 MILES IN 1 YEAR.

Not all reindeer pull Santa's sleigh. Most live in northern countries like Norway, Sweden, and Finland, and also North America, where they are also known as Caribou. They live together in herds (safety in numbers!) and travel large distances across very cold landscapes. In North America, they can migrate over 3,000 miles in 1 year and can travel as far as 23 miles in a single day. Also, newborn reindeer calves can walk usually within 90 minutes of being born. For a species that's always on the move, that's very useful!

100
MILES

ALMOST 10% OF A CAT'S BONES ARE IN ITS TAIL.

Most cats have long tails that they like to swish around, chase, and sometimes get in your face when you're trying to do something else. It's just what cats do. Their tails seem to have minds of their own, and the cat might not always be in control. But their tails are very important and help with balance and sensing what's around them. Adult cats have between 230 and 250 bones in their bodies (with an average of 244), and about 19 to 23 of these can be found in their tails. That's nearly one-tenth of all their bones! They need their tails for all kinds of things, so it makes sense that they would have so many bones to help them out.

99% OF A PANDA'S DIET IS BAMBOO.

Pandas, native to China, are fun, roly-poly animals that seem almost as round as anything else. For a long time, animal scientists weren't sure if they were actually bears or not, because they also are related to raccoons, but they decided that yes, pandas are bears. In the wild, pandas will eat almost nothing but bamboo. Thankfully, bamboo grows very fast (some species can grow 3 feet in a day!), so they always have enough to eat. They'll sometimes eat some kinds of grass or veggies, but bamboo is definitely their favorite snack, making up 99% of their diet!

99%

75%

50%

25%

0%

DOGS CAN SMELL UP TO 100,000 TIMES BETTER THAN HUMANS CAN.

We've all seen movies and TV shows where a dog is used to track someone who has run away or is lost. Sometimes they're given a piece of the person's clothing, and then they can track the scent that the person leaves behind. This is great for lost hikers and escaped prisoners, but is it really true? Actually, we're not quite sure how much better a dog can smell than a human. Some say it's between 10,000 and 100,000 times better. As one researcher put it, if a dog could, for example, see even 10,000 times better than us, "what you and I can see at a third of a mile, a dog could see more than 3,000 miles away and still see as well." So imagine how much better dogs can smell than we can!

100,000
TIMES
MORE

A TYPICAL HAMSTER CAN RUN UP TO 6 MILES A DAY ON A WHEEL.

If you've ever seen a hamster, you know that they love their wheels. They can get on those mini rides and run like crazy for a long time. These little creatures have a lot of energy that they need to work off, and as long as they're getting enough food and water, they will run a lot! Just how much? Well, a typical hamster can run up to 6 miles in a single day, which is kind of amazing when you think about it. And when they get tired, they'll stop. But don't expect them to rest too long before they get right back on that wheel again!

DAY 1

1 MILE

AN EMPEROR PENGUIN CAN SPEND UP TO 27 MINUTES UNDERWATER, HOLDING ITS BREATH.

Penguins need to dive into the ocean to catch their food (fish, of course!), and to be able to fish underwater, they need to be able to hold their breath for more than just a short while. And a species called the emperor penguin can hold its breath for a very long time. One study showed that they can hold their breath for up to 27 minutes, almost half an hour! How do they do it? Amazingly, they can take the oxygen they need from their muscles first, and their blood and lungs later. So they have different places to get the oxygen they need to stay underwater. When they come up, everything goes back to normal, and with luck, they have a tasty fish dinner!

TIME IN
MINUTES

ODDS AND ENDS

IN ANY GROUP OF 23 PEOPLE, THERE IS A 50% CHANCE THAT 2 OF THEM WILL HAVE THE SAME BIRTHDAY.

That doesn't seem like a lot of people, when you remember that there are 365 days in a year, but it's true. Mathematicians who have checked the numbers have found that there is an even chance that 2 people will share the same birthday in that small group. But it gets even more amazing. With a group 70 people, there is a 99.9% chance that 2 of them share the same birthday. See? Math can be fun!

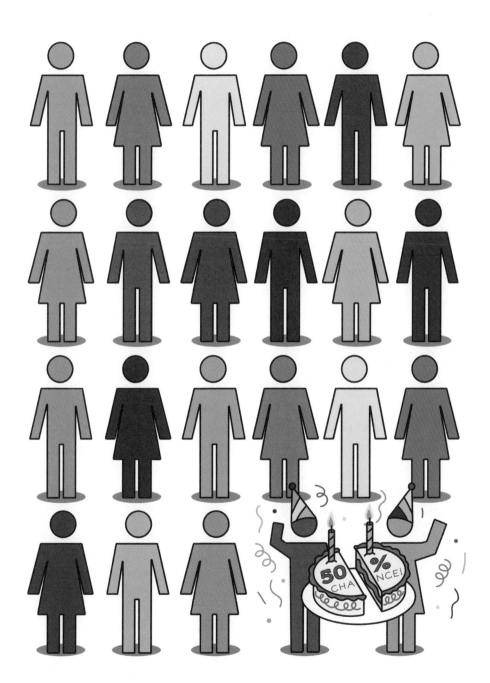

THE AVERAGE PERSON WILL SPEND ABOUT 25 TO 26 YEARS ASLEEP.

Some people need more sleep than others. One person might need 8 hours just to be able to get out of bed, while someone else might be fine with just 6. And of course, we all know someone who can sleep for like 12 hours with no problem! But did you know that average person will spend about one-third of their lives asleep? If you figure that people get about 8 hours a night, that's one-third of your day, which means about one-third of your life over the years. If you live to be 75 to 80 years, that's going to be about 25 to 26 years of your life spent sleeping!

THE AVERAGE PERSON HAS 67 DIFFERENT SPECIES OF BACTERIA LIVING IN THEIR BELLY BUTTON.

Some people in this study had as little as 29 species, while others had over 100! Okay, this just sounds gross, but it's not a weird or scary as you might think. In fact, our skin is covered with all kinds of bacteria that are actually good for us. They can prevent infections and help the body do what it needs to do very day. Our bodies have about as many bacteria cells in them, as "human" cells (it was once thought that we had a lot more bacteria than cells, actually). That's pretty amazing, and makes you wonder what we really are...

YOU LOSE ABOUT 50 TO 100 HAIRS A DAY.

People can lose hair for a lot of reasons: they might be sick, they might have a lot of stress, or they might just be getting older and are losing hair because it happens in their family. But believe it or not, it's normal for you to lose anywhere between 50 and 100 hairs a day. Every time you comb or brush your hair, or wash it, hair falls out. In a healthy person, new hair starts growing back right away, and since you have tens of thousands of hairs on your head, you never even notice that they're gone. So if you see a bunch of hairs in your comb or brush, don't freak out!

ONLY ABOUT 10-11% OF PEOPLE ARE LEFT-HANDED.

Left-handed people have had a rough time of things over history. Because there aren't that many of them, they have been seen as suspicious or even dangerous in the past, accused of being criminals, witches, and all sorts of other things. But left-handed people are just like everyone else, and it's silly to think otherwise. Being left-handed seems to be a combination of what they inherit from their parents, and possibly whether or not they were told not to use their left hands as babies and children. We do know that the two sides of the brain are better connected in left-handed people than right-handed, so that probably has something to do with it, which also makes them really cool!

OF PEOPLE ARE LEFT-HANDED!

11%

EYELASHES STAY AROUND FOR ABOUT 100 DAYS AND THEN FALL OUT.

Some people have really long eyelashes, while in some others, you almost don't notice them. Darkening them with mascara is not a new thing at all, by the way. Makeup was worn on the eyes by both men and women thousands of years ago. You have up to 150 eyelashes on the upper lid about 80 on the lower lid, and they typically stick around for about 3 months, or little more. Like your hair, they go through a growth cycle and then fall out, to be replaced by new ones. But since each lash does it at a different time, you never notice a change in their number or appearance.

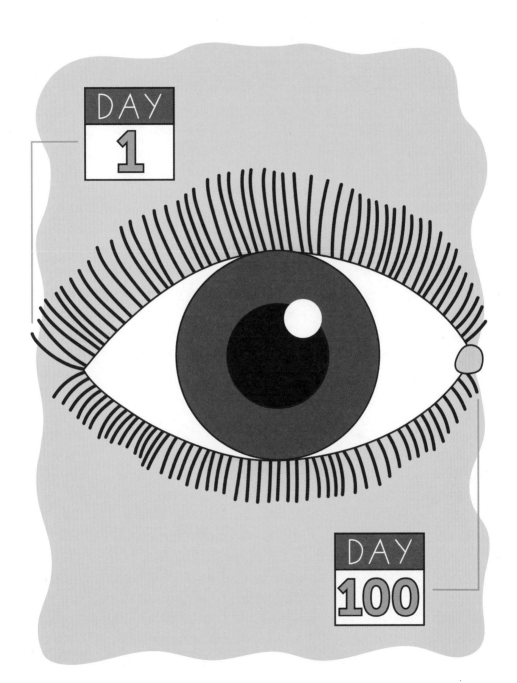

MOST PEOPLE FALL ASLEEP IN ABOUT 7 MINUTES.

There's more to it than this though. Studies have shown that after about 7 minutes, most people are in that dreamy state, where they're not really awake anymore, and may even have some dream-like hallucinations. But not every scientist thinks this qualifies as "sleep." It has to do with the kind of brain waves you're giving off, and to truly reach a sleeping state, and it might take another 5 minutes or so to drift into a light sleep. So the actual answer, it takes between 10 and 20 minutes to be completely asleep, but after 7 minutes, you're not really awake, either. Make sense?

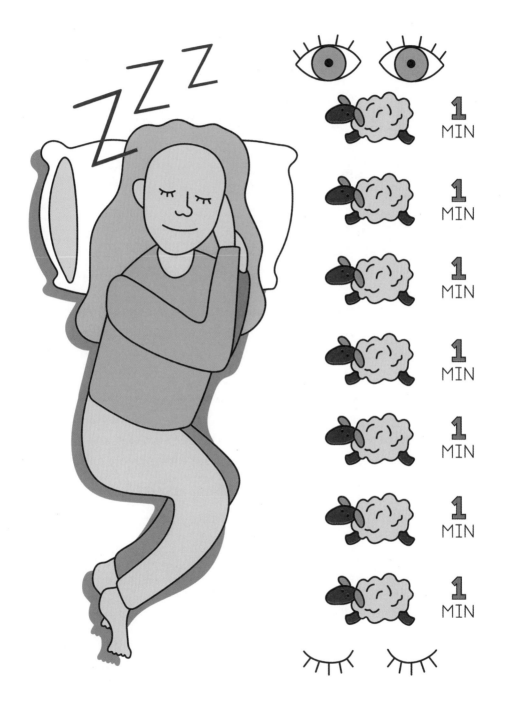

1 MIN

1 MIN

1 MIN

1 MIN

1 MIN

1 MIN

1 MIN

IT TAKES AROUND 50 LICKS TO FINISH 1 SCOOP OF ICE CREAM.

Just about everyone loves ice cream, and the more, the better! Whether you get a single scoop, a double, or a triple, it's guaranteed to make you smile, and maybe give you a headache if you try to eat it too fast! With that in mind, some people have wondered how long it takes to get through a single scoop. Well, assuming that you're not just gulping it down (and getting that headache), but are taking your time and licking it, it takes about 50 licks to finish off 1 scoop. It can take more if you want to make it last, but then it might melt. Try counting the next time you have an ice cream cone!

THE WORLD'S LONGEST FRENCH FRY WAS 34 INCHES.

We love French fries, but usually they're pretty small, right? Maybe 3 or 4 inches, so you can stuff several in your mouth at once? But French fries don't have to be that short, especially if they are curly fries. Back in 2010, a man named John Benbenek was eating curly fries from a food stand called Taffy's Hot Dog Stand in Buffalo, New York, when he noticed that a fry was super long. He carefully unrolled it and found that it was almost 3 feet, 34 inches to be exact! Since it was a spiral fry, it was cut from a single potato. He ended up not eating it, by the way, since it was collectible!

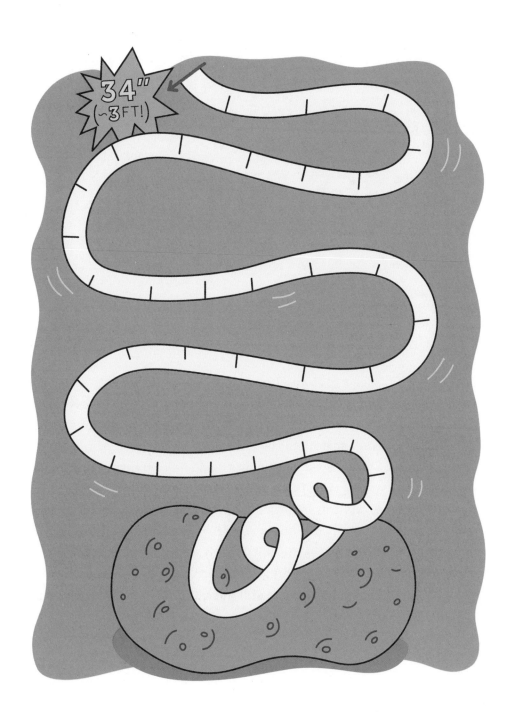

34"
(~3 FT!)

YOUR FINGERNAILS CAN GROW 4 TIMES FASTER THAN YOUR TOENAILS.

You might have noticed that you have to trim your fingernails a lot more often than you do your toenails. No, that's not just you; it's true for everybody. Fingernails really do grow faster than toenails, as much as 4 times as fast, in fact. But why? Well, scientists think it might be because of a couple of different reasons: Since we use our fingers much more than our toes (unless you're eating and writing with them, too!), there is more blood going to your fingers all the time, and this might cause the nails to grow faster. It might also be because of the way our fingers and toes are shaped and structured: the longer the bone, the faster the nail growth. So, your nails grow faster on your longer fingers, and since your fingers are longer than your toes, the nails grow faster, too. But strangely, we're still not quite sure why this happens.

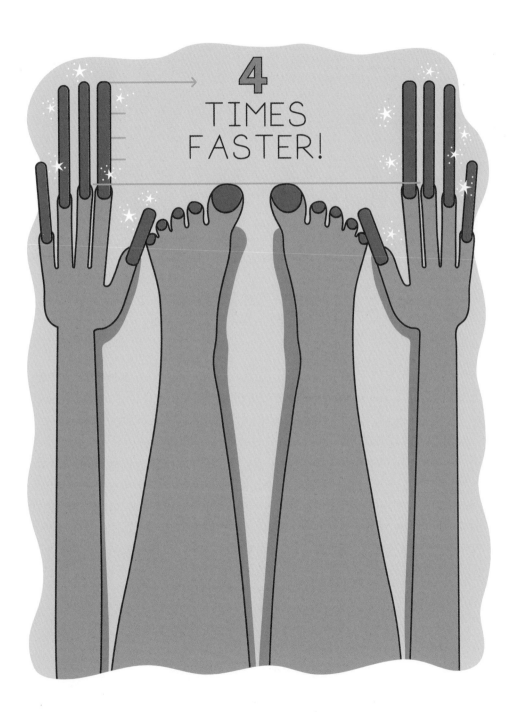

PEOPLE LIVING IN NORTH KOREA ARE ONLY ALLOWED TO HAVE 28 KINDS OF HAIRCUTS.

North Korea isn't exactly the most fun place to live. It's ruled by a dictator who seems to make some pretty cruel and crazy laws. And one of them is that the people of North Korea are only allowed to choose between 28 different hairstyles for themselves. If the look isn't on the list, you can't wear it. Men have 10 choices and women get 18 different styles to pick. No long hair for men (all the choices are for short hair), no purple or other colors, no mohawks or anything like that. The leader (who has his own hairstyle that no one else is allowed to have) says this is to keep out harmful influences from other countries, but it does seem pretty silly.

THE LARGEST NUMBER OF LEAVES EVER FOUND ON A CLOVER IS 56.

You might now that 4-leaf clovers are said to bring good luck, if you can find one (they're kind of rare). But did you know that clovers can have many more leaves than that? In May 2009, a farmer named Shigeo Obara in Hanamaki, Japan, discovered a clover in his field with an incredible 56 leaves! The *Guinness Book of World Records* was able to confirm that it did, indeed, have 56 leaves and is now the world record holder. Imagine the kind of good luck you might get from that!

3 LEAF CLOVER

4 LEAF CLOVER

56 LEAF CLOVER?!?!

SOURCES

GAMES AND SPORTS

1 NBC News
2 *Forbes*
3 PBS
4 Mental Floss
5 The Rubik Zone
6 Bleacher Report
7 *Wall Street Journal* and Politifact
8 Quora
9 *New York Daily News* and *Men's Journal*
10 Scout Life/Head's Up
11 Practical Golf
12 Bleacher Report
13 LiveAbout
14 The Vintage News
15 Neeness
16 Inning Ace
17 Reuters

TOYS

1 Bloomberg
2 Considerable
3 Grand View Research
4 Dicebreaker
5 Iti Manufacturing
6 Answers.com
7 Worldometer and UCTV
8 Barbiemedia.com
9 *Guinness World Records*
10 *Chicago Tribune*
11 Gizmodo

HISTORY

1 Quora
2 History.com
3 World History Encyclopedia
4 World Atlas
5 National Geographic
6 KQED
7 *The Morning Call* and Live Science
8 Delancey Place
9 All That's Interesting

SCIENCE

1 Healthline

2 Rapid Tables

3 University of Rochester Medical Center

4 United States Geological Survey

5 Perot Museum and Space.com

6 Nemours KidsHealth

7 American Museum of Natural History

8 Space.com

9 Healthgrades

10 The National Severe Storms Laboratory

11 The National Severe Storms Laboratory

12 National Weather Service

13 Space.com

14 NPR and Space.com

15 Planetary Science Institute

16 *New Scientist* and Space.com

ANIMALS

1 Mental Floss and *The Guardian*

2 National Geographic and Whales Online

3 Live Science and Treehugger

4 Medium and AZPetVet

5 Starkey and HeadStuff

6 Mental Floss

7 Kittyclysm and Chewy

8 National Geographic and the *Guinness Book of World Records*

9 PBS

10 Pocket Sized Pets

11 University of Bristol and Gizmodo

ODDS AND ENDS

1 *Scientific American* and Quora

2 *The Guardian*

3 National Geographic

4 American Academy of Dermatology

5 BBC

6 Lash Affair

7 Reverie

8 IceCream.com and the *Pittsburgh Post-Gazette*

9 World Record Academy

10 Medium and Dollar Shave Club

11 *Time* and *The Hindu Business Line*

12 *The Japan Times*

ABOUT THE AUTHOR

Tim Rayborn has written a large number of books and magazine articles (more than thirty each!), especially on subjects such as music, the arts, general knowledge, and history, though none of them are nearly as good as the classics in this book! He will no doubt write more. He lived in England for many years and studied at the University of Leeds, which means he likes to pretend that he knows what he's talking about. Incidentally, Statistics is the only college math class he got an A in, for what it's worth.

He's also an almost-famous musician who plays dozens of unusual instruments from all over the world that most people have never heard of and usually can't pronounce.

He has appeared on more than forty recordings, and his musical wanderings and tours have taken him across the U.S., all over Europe, to Canada and Australia, and to such romantic locations as Umbrian medieval towns, Marrakech, Vienna, Renaissance chateaux, medieval churches, and high school gymnasiums.

He currently lives in Northern California with many books, recordings, and instruments, and a sometimes-demanding cat. He's pretty enthusiastic about good wines and cooking excellent food.

timrayborn.com

ABOUT APPLESAUCE PRESS

Good ideas ripen with time. From seed to harvest, Applesauce Press creates books with beautiful designs, creative formats, and kid-friendly information. Like our parent company, Cider Mill Press Book Publishers, our press bears fruit twice a year, publishing a new crop of titles each spring and fall.

"Where Good Books Are Ready for Press"
Visit us online at
cidermillpress.com
or write to us at
12 Spring Street, PO Box 454
Kennebunkport, Maine 04046